mews
STYLE

mews
STYLE

sebastian deckker

Quiller Press

**The author and the publisher acknowledge with thanks
the following who have sponsored this book:**

Cadogan Estates

Grosvenor Estates

Howard de Walden Estates

First published 1998 by
Quiller Press Limited,
46 Lillie Road,
London SW6 1TN

Copyright © 1998
Sebastian Deckker

ISBN 1 899163 39 5

Jacket designed by Byron Abbott
Book designed by Jo Lee
Printed by Colorcraft Ltd.

previous page Woburn Mews
(now demolished).

acknowledgements

Special thanks go to my wife, Amanda, and my mother, Joan, for all their support and encouragement this last year; the publisher, Jeremy Greenwood; the photographer, Bill Burlington; and Stuart Corbyn at Cadogan Estates, without whom this book would not have been possible.

Also my thanks go to Dickie Arbiter (Director of Media Affairs at the Royal Collection), Andrew Ashenden (Howard de Walden Estates), Bective Davidson (Christopher Bective and Jeremy Davidson), Richard Bowden (Howard de Walden Estates), Colin and Jane Bothway, Toby Cholmeley, Ruth Eagleton-Grocott (*House and Garden*), Conrad Jameson, Antoine, Kati and Charlotte Lurot, David MacDonald (the Royal Borough of Kensington and Chelsea), Gillian Nunn (Cadogan Estates), the Hon Jane Roberts (Curator of the Print Room at Windsor Castle), Jane Sandars and the London team at Grosvenor Estates and Giles Worsley.

contents

foreword

by Stuart Corbyn

Property development and redevelopment in London in the eighteenth and nineteenth centuries was on a scale that few people would contemplate even today. The fact that large parts of the capital, including substantial areas on the Cadogan, Grosvenor and Howard de Walden Estates, retain their Georgian and Victorian characters is as much a reflection of the skills of the original architects and developers as the care and ingenuity of subsequent generations to adapt these buildings to suit contemporary requirements.

This applies in particular to mews houses, which started life as relatively humble buildings for coaches and coachmen but have developed a cachet of their own and have often evolved into sumptuous homes. However, because of the original purpose of these buildings, they were located in side streets and are only seen by those making a determined effort to do so.

Sebastian Deckker has had a particular fascination for mews houses for many years. His text, and Bill Burlington's photographs, illustrate the part these buildings have played in the development of a large part of London from a social as well as an architectural perspective. Their obvious enthusiasm for their subject brings to life often overlooked buildings and streets and should be a catalyst for those who take an interest in the built environment.

left Kynance Mews, painted by D.H. Lurot Betjeman, perfectly captures the rustic quality of the mews.

introduction

left and above Bathurst Mews – this long wide mews, typical of the Paddington area, is home to the Hyde Park Riding Stables – "London's oldest original riding stables." It is named after Elizabeth Bathurst of Clarendon Park in Wiltshire who had married a member of the wealthy and influential Frederick family of the Manor of Paddington and was recently featured in *Scandal*, the film about the notorious John Profumo affair.

"The mews of London constitute a world of their own." – Henry Mayhew

This observation was true even before it was written in 1851. All that has changed today is how that "world" is occupied.

Mews style is about a way of life, both past and present. It is quintessentially English yet intensely urban and as much a part of London tradition as Trooping the Colour, the red Routemaster bus, black taxis and Harrods. Unfortunately, this labyrinth of cobbled streets, that weave their clandestine path through the capital, is so often forgotten. Unlike the noble houses they once served, which for the most part have remained in residential use, the mews have had constantly to adapt to keep pace with the new demands of their occupants. The change is apparent in their names: from Lancaster Stables to Belsize Court Garages, only a scant number still evoke their equestrian past – Saddle Mews, Horse Shoe Yard and Cheval Place; their inhabitants: from servants' quarters to bachelor pads, oozing with sex appeal, for playboys and the Jet-Set and more recently for secluded family homes by the wealthy; their use: from stables and coach-houses to car workshops, studios for a surfeit of designers and artists, probably the only exception being the Hyde Park Riding Stables in Bathurst Mews; and their status: from the downtrodden and impoverished to the socially acceptable and affluent.

below Belsize Court Garages.

above Ledbury Mews North.

above middle Prince's Mews.

above Colville Mews.

Variety within the mews itself supplements this unique environment. Traces of the past are blended with elements of the present. A plethora of styles can be seen existing side by side – old and new, traditional and modern, modest and ornate. However, it is the interaction of people in the mews that provides us with the most noticeable diversification. Unlike the architecture of the main squares and streets that was designed to be studied; its proportions investigated, the fine detailing scrutinised and their use of materials admired, the mews were essentially built on a more human (or equine) scale. They were never intended to be seen from afar, being purely functional, but to be occupied, whether by the horse and carriage or nowadays by children playing in the street, dogs being walked, cyclists escaping the congestion and pollution of the main roads, cars being washed or owners simply relaxing with friends outside their house. The transition of the mews is as diverse as the properties they contain and it is this remarkable character that will be exposed.

below Mount Row.

middle left Pembroke Mews.

left St Luke's Mews.

right In 1990, Jean-Louis Dumas-Hermès, President of Hermès, the exclusive French luxury goods company, and the fifth generation descendant of the founder, Thierry Hermès, visited London and the Royal Mews. Mr Dumas-Hermès was "enchanted by the tradition of the Royal Mews, the beauty and craftsmanship of its coaches and of course by its long-standing association with horses."[1] He realised immediately that this would be the perfect subject for a Hermès scarf and appointed the designer Colonel de Fougerolle, who had previously worked with Hermès on a number of occasions, to implement a suitable interpretation. De Fougerolle was also "inspired by the wealth of possibilities" and, appropriately in Hermès' *Year of the Horse*, the Royal Mews scarf was conceived. Mr Dumas-Hermès later had the honour to present it to Her Majesty The Queen at the Royal Windsor Horse Show in May 1993.

1 Hermès, *The Royal Mews* – A story of a scarf

overview

origin

Mention the word "mews" in the media or, more recently, property supplements and estate agents' sales particulars, and a definite image is conjured up. It is probably of a narrow cobbled lane, tucked out of sight and mind behind the grand and imposing houses that make up the elegant squares, terraces and streets of Georgian and Victorian London. These are the very same squares, terraces and streets that can be seen in the recent spate of period dramas, and even musicals such as *Oliver*. It is ironic that in these productions the actual mews are never seen – left only to the imagination and the fact that the set is generally overrun with horses, carriages and grooms. It is only when the mews became popular, towards the end of the twentieth century, that they are depicted – in *The Avengers, The Saint* – and with one of the most coveted icons of the eighties, the VW Golf, with their true Union Jack colours. The small, but charming, cottages feature a staggering array of styles and finishes – some brightly painted and preserved, others left unadorned and unloved. Peace and relative tranquillity are only a moment away from the hustle and bustle of the main thoroughfares. More practically for some potential mews-dwellers, it is the garage that is the attraction; in a city overrun with traffic (and traffic wardens), these former stables and coach-houses provide a private and secure parking space that has proved to be both invaluable and extremely popular.

right Doughty Mews.

above Osten Mews.

left St Luke's Mews.

The term "mews" first appears in connection with the Royal Mews when it was originally situated at Charing Cross, on the site of the present National Gallery in Trafalgar Square. This was where the royal falcons were formally "mewed" or left to shed their plumage. After a fire in 1537 destroyed his stables in Bloomsbury, Henry VIII turned the Royal Mews into the Royal Stables (although the title of Royal Mews was kept). The birds were evicted and, after some enlargement and reorganisation, the horses, together with the itinerant stable staff and grooms, were installed in their new residence. This new generic term of stables and coach-houses being referred to as "mews" came to be well known in the seventeenth century, increasing in popularity for the next two hundred and fifty years.

above St Anselm's Place – it is the garage that is the attraction, depending on the size of the car of course!

above Upper Montagu Mews in 1915.

above Prince's Mews.

above Chippenham Mews.

Subsequently, mews were identified as being "a set of stabling round an open yard, now often converted into dwellings."[2]

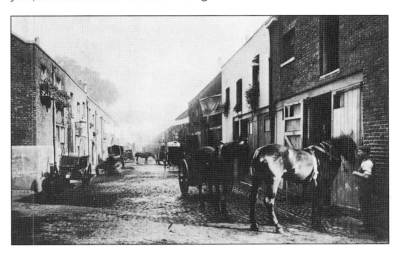

left Keppel Mews South in 1900 (demolished in 1901).

After the decline of the horse and carriage at the end of the nineteenth century and the emergence of the motor-car as a popular and easily accessible means of transport, the need to keep stables diminished. After a period of unpopularity and dilapidation, they became an ideal solution for those looking for a house, albeit on the slightly cramped side, in the fashionable areas of London where most of the properties fronting the squares and streets were being converted into flats and maisonettes. What these cottages lacked in convenience they certainly made up for in novelty.

left Linden Mews.

2 Definition from the *Oxford English Dictionary*

These "bijou" homes in the mews further developed in the Swinging Sixties out of the culture of the car where anything from the classic Fiat 500 or Mini to the elegant Aston Martin and powerful E-Type were stowed away. The same principle that had once kept these lanes from the public eye – set off the main street and cunningly hidden behind narrow openings or grandiose arches – is exactly why they appeal to their new inhabitants today. Driving into a mews, one has the impression of being transported into a very rural setting, travelling down a cobbled street surrounded by brightly painted cottages with overflowing terracotta pots and hanging baskets of flowers decorating the often humble façades. The sound of hooves and carriage wheels on the cobbles has now been replaced by the purr of engines.

below Duchess Mews.

"Flowers in pots on window sills, or massed in large tubs flanking the front door, are a prominent feature."[3]

left Kersley Mews.

There is, however, a another interpretation of the word "mews" that has evolved only recently. This is the trend for "mews style" developments – a phrase applied by builders and planners to attract purchasers (even though the properties have had nothing at all to do with horses). They recall a bygone age, an age which evokes a community spirit long since forgotten. They generally consist of low-built houses, each with a garage, set round a secure courtyard. The scale is essentially more human and generally more compatible than the typical suburban scene, without the obvious drawbacks of their predecessors.

left Belgrave Mews West.

But how did this now familiar urban composition emerge? For the answer, we must look back as far as 1066.

3 Gordon Mackenzie, *Marylebone – Great City north of Oxford Street,* 1972

estates

After the Norman Conquest, much of the land now occupied by London's West End was granted to the followers of William the Conqueror who in turn bestowed it upon various religious institutions such as the Abbey of Westminster. With the Dissolution of the monasteries in 1535-9, vast holdings of monastic land were confiscated by Henry VIII who then sold, leased or gave away smaller plots to his loyal courtiers and the aristocracy. Thus, London differed significantly from other cities outside the British Isles in its pattern of land ownership being divided not into remote and individual freeholds but into, often substantial, landed estates. Another factor in the emergence of these estates was the increased economic activity and the growing wealth and prosperity of a small number of middle-class landowners, generally manufacturers and merchants. The landowners included the Russells, Cavendishes, Wriothesleys and Grosvenors. By the beginning of the seventeenth century, most of central London was owned by private families. This concentration of land possession in the hands of relatively few families enabled them to exert an immense control over the capital's fortune.

above Devonshire Close.

left Cavendish Mews North.

The owners of these estates were in the fortunate and unique position of possessing land which had either been passed on by Henry VIII, accumulated by business acumen or acquired through prudent marriages. These noble families, who had once built great manor houses in the country as a sign of their wealth and status, now turned to London to create a lasting impression of their importance on the capital. Even today, it is possible to discover the legacy of these distinguished families whose titles and country seats are kept alive in the names of the squares, streets and mews of London.

right Bloomsbury Square in 1727.

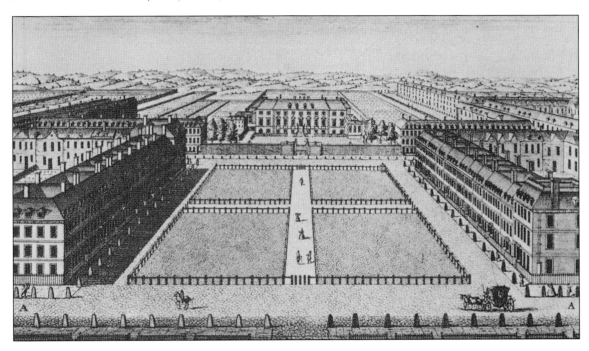

The first of the big estates to be developed belonged to the Russell family, whose ancestor John, the first Earl of Bedford, had been granted the Covent Garden area, north of the Strand, by Henry VIII. After a proclamation by Elizabeth I in 1580 about the construction of "any newe Building or Buildings House or Houses for habitation", an Act was passed in 1592. Thereafter, in order to prevent any undesirable development, a detailed plan of the proposed development had to be submitted and a building licence obtained. In 1631, Charles I gave permission to the fourth Earl of Bedford for the demolition of the existing buildings on the site. Bedford subsequently engaged the king's architect, Inigo Jones (1573-1651), to realise the housing project – "the first great contribution to English urbanism"[4]. The *piazza,* designed as

4 Sir John Summerson, *Georgian London,* 1991, page 29

13

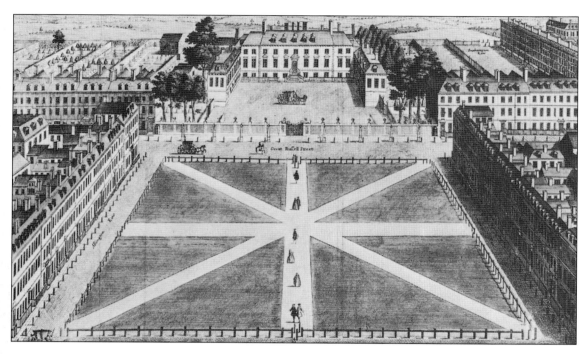

right Charing Cross in 1682, from a map by William Morgan, showing Blew Mews, Green Mews and the appropriately named Dunghill Mews.

above Bloomsbury Square in 1746.

a complete unit with accommodation for all classes of society, rich and poor, was reminiscent of the *Place des Vosges* (formally the *Place Royale*) built by Henri IV in Paris. According to Sir John Summerson:

> ...we owe Covent Garden to three parties: Charles I, with his fine taste and would-be autocratic control of London's architecture; Jones with his perfectly mature understanding of Italian design; and the Earl of Bedford with his business-like aptitude for speculative building.[5]

The next important step was taken by Thomas Wriothesley, the fourth Earl of Southampton, just after the Restoration, with his development in Bloomsbury. Bloomsbury Square became not only the prototype of the classical London square – "a little town"[6] – but was also the first residential unit to be developed in conjunction with speculative builders. The Bedford and Bloomsbury estates were brought together in 1669 when Southampton's daughter married the son and heir of the fifth Earl and first Duke of Bedford.

This phase of London's evolution was halted abruptly with two tragedies: the Great Plague (1665) and the Great Fire (1666). The mews, in their present form, were only created when London began to expand northwards and westwards into the arable and pasture land, as yet undeveloped, owned by

5 Sir John Summerson, *Georgian London*, 1991, page 30

6 Taken from John Evelyn's diary dated the 9th February 1665

a new breed of landlord. The precedent set by the Earls of Bedford and Southampton was now taken up, and perfected, by the careful and imaginative planning of other hereditary landlords who are, in part, responsible for the configuration of London today.

The first of this series of developments was executed in 1717 by the first Earl of Scarborough when he planned and built Hanover Square. At the same time, a young patron and follower of the new Palladian movement was developing an area behind his house in Piccadilly.[7] The third Earl of Burlington, who had obtained an Act of Parliament permitting him to build on Ten Acre Close, was a enthusiastic amateur architect and an important promoter, along with William Kent and Giacomo Leoni, of classical architecture.

Other estates formed in this period of expansion include Grosvenor in the 1720s, Portland (Cavendish Harley) in the 1730s and an area of Marylebone owned by Henry Portman in the 1750s.

At the beginning of the eighteenth century, the Mayfair segment of the Grosvenor Estate was merely a collection of fields, known as "The Hundred Acres", bounded by what is now Oxford Street to the north and Park Lane to the west. It had been passed to Sir Thomas Grosvenor after his marriage to Mary Davies. In 1710, their son, Sir Richard Grosvenor, obtained the Act allowing him to grant leases on Grosvenor Fields, although no development was begun until 1721. By now, the area around Hanover Square was well established and formed the necessary communication links to the new Grosvenor Estate development. The building work, which included a grand square, was planned by the estate's agent, Robert Andrews, certainly in collaboration with the baronet. Surrounding the square, there were the main secondary streets and behind these, the mews. In 1746, Roque's map shows a number of "mewse" located around Grosvenor Square including Shepherd's, Reeve's, Adam's, Blackburn's, Wood's and Three Kings Yard. The design of the square was influenced by Burlington, and indeed Colen Campbell prepared a drawing for the east side, with the façades of the houses being treated in such a way that they gave the visual impression of being one magnificent and extended palace. When it was completed, it was noted for being the grandest square in London.

Another estate was destined for a similar treatment. This was an area of land north of Oxford Street and to the west of Lord Southampton's Bloomsbury estate and, again, strategically placed in the path of London's continuing expansion. Development here was also set in motion by a marriage – in 1713, between Edward Harley, son of Robert Harley, first Earl of Oxford and Mortimer, and

7 Now the Royal Academy

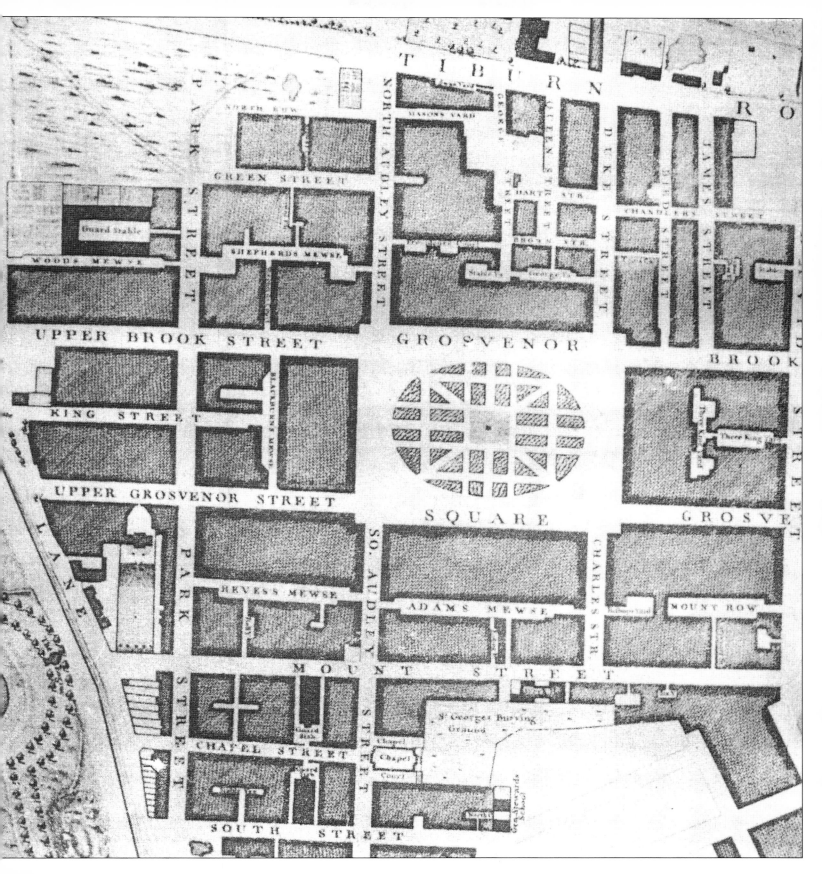

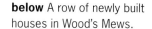

Henrietta Cavendish Holles, daughter of the late John Holles, Duke of Newcastle, who had purchased the manor of Marylebone in 1708 for £17,500.

Harley, himself titled Baron Harley of Wigmore, was a wealthy and educated man with all the business and architectural acumen for becoming a developer. The initial project was for the area around Cavendish Square and the ambitious plan, published in 1719 by the estate surveyor, John Prince, followed the now well established set pattern of a central square with streets, including mews, leading

above Harley Place – note the two previous titles.

below A grand building with a clock tower and arched passage at the end of Three Kings Yard.

left Adam's Row (known as Adam's Mews until 1937) with its ornate gables and decorative finials.

below A row of newly built houses in Wood's Mews.

off it with a church and a market. The streets and mews were named after the family and its connections, a practice which was continued when Edward and Henrietta's only child, Margaret Cavendish Harley, married William Bentinck, second Duke of Portland in 1734. The Harley Estate then became the Portland Estate, remaining in the hands of the Portland family until the death of the fifth Duke of Portland in 1879. He died unmarried and the Estate passed jointly to his two sisters, Charlotte, Viscountess Ossington, and Lucy Joan Cavendish-Bentinck, widow of the sixth Lord Howard de Walden. After Charlotte's death in 1889 the title to the Estate passed fully to the Howard de Walden family with whom it has remained ever since.

Although development on the Portman Estate was considered as early as the 1750s, it was not until 1768 that any construction was carried out in Portman Square, which proved very successful. The delay was due to another property slump in London starting with the South Sea Bubble and lasting until the end of the Seven Years War in 1763. However, the next thirty years, until the Napoleonic Wars, are what Summerson referred to as the "golden age" of London building.

One of the last estates to emerge in the eighteenth century was the Manor of Chelsea along the north bank of the river Thames. Before any major works were carried out in 1771, the ownership of the land followed a convoluted path. It had been owned by the Cheyne family after the Civil War. In 1685, the manor passed to William Cheyne who, having planned Cheyne Row in 1708, sold it to Sir Hans Sloane. After Sloane's death, the manor was divided between his two daughters who subsequently married – Sarah to George Stanley and Elizabeth to Charles Cadogan. Further development was planned and carried out by the architect, Henry Holland, called Hans Town which included a large house, called Sloane Place or "The Pavilion", for himself. Sadly, this has since been demolished, remembered only in the wide mews running parallel to Sloane Street, Pavilion Road.

With this increased development and expansion, better lines of communication had to be provided to prevent congestion. One such scheme was the construction of the New Road (the present Marylebone and Euston Roads). The New Road came at exactly the right time for the estates to the north, particularly the Bedford Estate. The challenge was taken up by the fourth Duke of Bedford who was familiar with classical architecture and had acquired a sympathy for the classical planning in Bath. Unfortunately, Bedford died in 1771 and it was left to his widow to carry on with the scheme that her husband had been so passionate about. This she did with the help of the London agent, Robert Palmer, and in 1774 Bedford Square was started. When completed, it "ushered in a new era of elegance and discipline in Georgian town planning".[8]

below Pavilion Road.

below A bollard, surviving from 1819, in Pavilion Road denoting the boundary of Hans Town.

8 Simon Jenkins, *The Landlords of London,* page 55

right above and below Cheyne Mews.

right Grosvenor Cottages.

At the beginning of the nineteenth century two further estates were planned and developed. They have one factor in common: the architect, George Basevi. Whilst we have previously seen the construction of houses in Mayfair, it was now the turn of the land behind Grosvenor Place – the Belgravia section of the vast Grosvenor Estate. This land lay just to the east of Henry Holland's Hans Town.

It was Thomas Cubitt, the builder, who had been previously responsible for building in parts of Bloomsbury just north of Bedford Square and who had originally taken a lease of the "five fields" belonging to Lord Grosvenor,

left An aerial view of Hans Town and Belgravia.

although the responsibility had been passed to Basevi for the construction of Belgrave Square. Cubitt's work can be seen elsewhere on the estate in the construction of Eaton Square, begun in 1827 and named after the Grosvenor's country seat, Eaton Hall in Cheshire. The land surrounding these squares was, like their eighteenth-century predecessors, laid out by Thomas Cundy with adjacent secondary streets and abundant mews and included services such as drainage, lighting and sewerage.

In 1829, Basevi was appointed by the Trustees of Henry Smith's Charity, whose names litter the estate today, as architect for the development of the South Kensington Estate. Although classical, it was on a much smaller scale than his previous commission in Belgravia. The estate was founded by Henry Smith, later a "gentleman and citizen of London". On his death in 1628, his will bequeathed that part of the estate should be used to purchase land, the income from which should be used both for "the use of poore captives being slaves under the Turkish pirate" and for "the use and reliefe of the poorest of my kindred". The site acquired, approximately eighty-five acres, is slightly extended and sprawling in nature, and remains almost unchanged since the last of the original trustees died in 1668. It is roughly divided into two sections: to the west it is bounded by Fulham Road, Old Brompton Road, Pelham Street and Cranley Mews/Thistle Grove, to the east the estate is marked by Brompton Road, Walton Street and Yeomans Row, and is between Lennox Gardens Mews, Pont Street, Milner Street and the west side of Clabon

right Cranley Mews.

Mews, the east side being owned by the Cadogan Estate. William Clutton was appointed the estate surveyor in 1769 and in 1772 the trustees were granted an Act allowing them to grant building leases on the estate. The architect, Michael Novosielski, was one of the first to take advantage of the Act and it was hoped that the development would attract a similar class of tenant as neighbouring Hans Town. The estate was further developed by a number of builders up to 1851, the year of the Great Exhibition, and beyond. Like so many of the estates, planning, development and redevelopment were continually being adapted, the process dictated by the demands of their inhabitants.

below A very unusual treatment of a house in Clabon Mews.

below left The entrance to Avenue Studios in Sydney Close. Baron Marochetti, a local resident, converted a stable, in what used to be called Sydney Mews, into a "sculpture room" shortly after the Great Exhibition in 1851. In 1870 the remaining coach-houses and stables in the mews were rebuilt to form a complex of artists' studios.

left Clareville Grove Mews.

As well as these large estates, there were numerous smaller developments being carried out in London often comprising as little as one or two streets, some even with mews. They, however, also made a contribution to the general expansion of the city. If the landowners of these minor developments are at one end of the scale, then surely at the other end must be the development planned by George IV, the Prince Regent. The project – Marylebone Park, which had reverted back to the Crown in 1811; the architect – John Nash (1752-1835). The Prince Regent would be, out of all the landowners

above and right Gloucester Gate Mews.

already developing their estates, the most wealthy, most cultured, most travelled and most sophisticated, as was to be expected of the future King. It was certainly conceived, in 1812, as a grand project which involved building a number of detached villas, set in their own grounds, in the park, introducing a canal, constructing a great circus bisected by the New Road and designing a "Royal Mile" along Regent Street from the Park to Carlton House.

However the project was dogged with financial problems and was never realised to its full potential or grandeur. Today Regent's Park is only a shadow of its original design – a number of detached villas, the classical terraces on the east and west sides of the Park, begun in 1820, and half of the circus (Park Crescent) facing what is now Oxford Street. Behind the ornate terraces that line the Park – among them Cumberland, Gloucester, Chester, Hanover and Cambridge – there were numerous mews planned, although very few remain in their original state today, and even the mews[9] behind Park Crescent are substantially altered. Summerson captured the scene as:

> Carved pediments, rich in allegory, top the trees; massive pavilions, standing forward like the corps de garde of Baroque chateaux, are linked to the main structures by triumphal arches or columnar screens; each terrace stretches its length in all the pride of unconfined symmetry. It is magnificent. And behind it all – behind it are the rows and rows of identical houses, identical in their narrowness, their thin pretentiousness, their poverty of design. Where the eye apprehends a mansion of great distinction, supported by lesser mansions and service quarters, the mind must interpret it as a block of thin houses, with other blocks of thin houses carrying less ornament or none at all. The sham is flagrant and absurd.[10]

We shall return to the work of John Nash in more detail later in the book for his important role in two further projects: his construction of Carlton House Terrace with the stables that served it, Carlton Mews, and the building of the Royal Mews situated in the grounds of Buckingham House (renamed Buckingham Palace in 1821).

All these developments follow a similar pattern – a strategy perfected by the landlords of these great estates who had now seen their once idle land beautifully planned and refined, and the houses in the squares and streets rented, a large proportion to the gentry and aristocracy. This large-scale development would not have been possible without the continuing refinement of the leasehold system. The richest landlords, even if they had wished to part with their land in the first place, could not have financed a project such as Grosvenor Square. This was left to the new breed of entrepreneur – the building speculator – to take on the risk and it is they who were responsible for the growing cultivation and gentrification of London.

9 Park Crescent Mews East and Park Crescent Mews West

10 Sir John Summerson, *Georgian London*, 1991, page 182

leaseholds

This new structure of land tenure came about for a number of reasons. Firstly, there was a growing need for expansion in the seventeenth and eighteenth centuries. The land that lay in London's westward path was owned, as we have seen, by wealthy and influential noblemen who had acquired these estates by various means. Secondly, these individuals, who were often well travelled and familiar with classical architecture, were keen to develop their estates in a way that would bring glory and distinction on their families for future generations without destroying their integrity by selling the land outright. However, possessing neither the finances nor the inclination for actually building themselves, they divided their land into smaller plots which were sold to speculators who would build the houses at their own expense. Thus the problem was solved. These innovative ground landlords were able to retain overall control of ownership whilst dictating the architectural style and social status of the area, thus reducing any financial risk to a minimum. Thirdly, it allowed the adaptation of the estate, as a complete unit, when fashions and ideas changed, being in the hands of a single freeholder, rather than a multitude of individual owners, who could re-evaluate the situation when the leases expired.

below Mount Row.

above Onslow Mews West, **centre** Redcliffe Mews and **centre below** Pavilion Road provide excellent examples of new developments.

This process, re-established with Lord Southampton's development in Bloomsbury, in which the speculative builder was instrumental, dominates the character of London. The city, having been never contrived, is a series of hedonistic town planning exercises that make up the whole, each with its own identity, an identity stimulated by the policies of the individual ground landlords who, in turn, reflected their own interpretation of the estate. This procedure is still very much in evidence today. Initially, a landowner, in conjunction with the estate surveyor or architect, had to apply for a building licence and submit a detailed plan of the proposed scheme. This plan would also be used to convey the essence of the scheme to possible investors or speculators by setting out strict specifications for infrastructure, elevations, plans, construction, dimensions and decorative style. Once a speculator had declared an interest in purchasing land for development, a building agreement was drawn up defining the exact area and standard of construction and the terms of the lease, which would include the amount of ground rent payable, lease length and any other relevant covenants or conditions. Although not many green-field sites exist in London today, each estate still has its own policies about property development – policies that have not altered significantly since the eighteenth century. Now, however, the ground landlord is not at the top of the chain, and the estate plans have to be drawn up in accordance with a number of regulatory organisations which include English Heritage, the Secretary of State and the local Planning Authority.

It might transpire that the plots were either sold to individual speculators, constructing only one or two houses, or a master-builder, who would be responsible for the whole site. Whichever the case, before a building lease could be granted, the houses, on completion, had to meet with the approval of the estate surveyor who would check that the property had been erected in accordance with the building agreement. The leaseholder would then have to keep the property in an appropriate state of repair as set out in the lease and there were severe penalties for failing to do so. The ground landlord also had the power to prevent the introduction of any structural or occupational alterations being carried out by the lessee, to the extent of forfeiting the lease and evicting the leaseholder. Originally leases were very short, as little as 42 years in Bloomsbury Square, although by the end of the eighteenth century they had increased to 99 years, which became the standard (although some are shorter today). One critic of the short lease was Isaac Ware who, in his *Complete Body of Architecture* (1756), expressed concern that buildings were not made to last beyond the term of the lease and indeed "some have carried the art of slight building so far, that their houses have fallen down before they were tenanted". This statement, for the most part, has been disproved.

Effectively, the leasehold system benefited the landowner, great or small, who had seen his land, at no expense to himself, transformed from open fields to open squares and streets. It was the landlord who had even devised the layout to his own taste; it was the landlord who subsequently collected the invariably increasing rents, no matter what the state of the prevailing property market; it was to the landlord that the houses reverted back at the end of the lease and it was the landlord who was keen to maintain and preserve the quality of the area for the future prosperity of his descendants. In total contrast, it was the speculator who took the risk: to build houses at minimum

left Wilton Row – many of the mews houses in Belgravia are still held on leases from the Grosvenor Estate.

expense for maximum return, whilst constructing the right type of house suitable for the location and abiding by the conditions of the stringent building agreements and leases. The speculator was also left exposed by factors outside his control, not only economic and political, but the threat of war. It is clear however that, despite Nash's remark that "speculative building would be the death of English architecture", the often forgotten speculator has contributed a great deal to the elegance and character of London.

speculators

In order to see the evolution of this class of builder and their effect on the growth of the mews house, we must look back to the emergence of the great estates which undertook the majority of the development in the seventeenth, eighteenth and early nineteenth centuries. While some speculators have become household names, synonymous with grand and elegant schemes, others, lacking in skill and self-promotion, have, like their projects, been forgotten.

There is no clear definition of a speculative builder – it might be anybody "from a peer to a labourer"[11] or indeed, an architect to a craftsman. It did not even require great wealth, just a sound business knowledge and the ability to reach an equilibrium between what was fashionable and what would sell. We have already seen that Lord Southampton was the first landowner to introduce the speculative builder as an intermediary in the development of his Bloomsbury Estate, an action that would soon snowball and be responsible for a great number of similar schemes that followed.

One of the estates we have looked at belonged to Edward Harley. His surveyor was John Prince who not only prepared a lavish plan for the estate, but was also a speculator in his own right and had actually taken a large site on the south side of Cavendish Square for this purpose. He even named a street after himself. Harley was also supported by the architect, James Gibbs. Another estate of a similar vintage was that owned by Sir Richard Grosvenor and although Grosvenor Square was a grand project, it is not until the land,

left Hippodrome Mews.

11 Sir John Summerson, *Georgian London*, 1991, page 42

now Belgravia and Pimlico, was developed that we see an abundance of speculative builders, responsible not only for laying out these areas, but for other estates in increasingly fashionable west London.

1774 was a date particularly relevant to the speculator as it witnessed the introduction of the London Building Act. The Act was introduced to standardise building procedure, setting out explicit policies about materials, construction, "for the further and better Regulation of Building and Party Walls; and for the more effectually preventing Mischief by Fire", as it attempted to update and consolidate the numerous Acts since the Fire of London. It also set out four "rates" for houses, each having its own set requirements. But whilst it set a benchmark for architectural design, some felt that it was responsible for both "inexpressible monotony" and mediocrity. This, however, seen from the point of view of the landlord or builder, is unfortunately what any new legislation tends to achieve.

1774 also saw the construction of Bedford Square – the second phase of development on the Bedford Estate. It was in association with Robert Palmer, the Bedfords' agent, that saw the arrival of Thomas Leverton, William Scott and Robert Grews and the success of the entire project. Apart from the grand houses in the square, they also contracted to lay out the necessary infrastructure and to build a number of coach-houses and stables behind. It was intended that Bedford Square should become a "focal point for a whole new network of streets and mews."[12] The only evidence of this project today is Gower Mews.

The Bedford Estate also introduced Henry Holland, then the Duke's surveyor, whose work on the Cadogan Estate has already been discussed, James Burton (1761-1837), who would later build York Terrace, Cornwall Terrace and Clarence Terrace in Regent's Park, was responsible for a great part of the Bedford Estate which included the development of Russell Square, and, the already celebrated Thomas Cubitt – "the king of developers" (1788-1855), whose schemes, along with those of his younger brother, Lewis, we shall see not only in Bloomsbury but in their greatest and best known project centred around the Grosvenor Estate – the transformation of Belgravia and Pimlico. Burton had also agreed, along with his building work in Bloomsbury and Russell Squares, to build a number of mews including Tavistock Mews, which was subsequently demolished in 1897. The same fate awaited Southampton Mews and Montague Mews between 1898-9.

Cubitt now turned part of his attention to the estate owned by the second Marquess of Westminster, and although the site, extending to some nineteen

12 Donald J Olsen, *Town Planning in London,* 1982, page 48

acres included what is now Belgrave Square, it was Eaton Square, started in 1827, which was built by Thomas and Lewis Cubitt. It is possible to see today the number of mews that served Eaton Square, the majority laid out by the Cubitts. These include Eaton Mews North, Eaton Mews South, Eaton Mews West, Boscobel Place and Eccleston Mews. These two squares were only part of a larger plan, partly devised by James Wyatt, and prepared by the estate's surveyor, Thomas Cundy, brother of Joseph Cundy, who had been responsible for the development of Chester Square. This square shares, with Eaton Square, the mews in Eaton Mews South and Boscobel Place, and there is a further range to the south and east, being Ebury Mews and Chester Square Mews respectively. We have already seen that the architect, George Basevi, had been handed the responsibility of laying out and constructing Belgrave Square, on which work had started in 1826. This was another grand square and justifiably served with numerous mews houses for the residents, being Belgrave Mews North, Belgrave Mews South, Belgrave Mews West and Belgrave Mews East (now Montrose Place). Just to the north, work began in 1827 on Wilton Crescent along with the mews, Wilton Crescent Mews (now Wilton Row), and the vast assortment of alleys and yards off the present Kinnerton Street. Wilton Row is adjacent to the present complex of Grosvenor Crescent Mews.

The self-contained mews block, as a defined architectural element, established by the Grosvenor Estate in Mayfair, was perfected in Belgravia.

right Old Barrack Yard linking Wilton Row to Knightsbridge showing the entrance and the original granite sett paving.

left The Chelsea Pottery in Ebury Mews.

Pimlico, which once occupied the southern tip of the Grosvenor Estate, was Cubitt's next scheme and was one of the biggest projects to be planned by a single developer. It was based around Warwick Square and Eccleston Square, which formed the centre of an extremely ordered pattern of streets, forming an easily recognisable grid. Although visually stunning, with the austere stucco-fronted houses, it is now in the unfortunate position of being referred to as the "poor man's Belgravia". There are also mews to be found here, Warwick Square Mews, Hugh Mews, West Mews and Eccleston Square Mews, but they are separated from the main squares, unlike in Belgravia, and are no longer connected to any particular house.

above Hugh Mews.

After the death in 1795 of Michael Novosielski, one of the first builders on Henry Smith's Charity Estate in South Kensington and responsible for the construction of some seventy-seven houses, the next major development was carried out by George Basevi, who had already established his reputation in Belgravia when he was appointed as architect for the estate in 1829, along with the principle builder, James Bonnin. In a building agreement drawn up in 1833, Pelham Crescent was constructed followed by Pelham Place and Pelham Road, named after Henry Pelham, one of the estate's trustees. Although built by Bonnin, the work was constantly supervised by Basevi and his designs remain a dominant influence on the style of the properties in the area.

After his death, the development of the estate was dominated by one man, Charles James Freake and, as the wording on his Blue Plaque commemorates, a "Builder and Patron of the Arts". Between 1845 and the mid-1880s, he was responsible for the construction of a great number of houses, as well as separate coach-houses and stables on the estate. Amongst the most prominent developments were those of Onslow Square, Onslow Gardens, Sumner Place, Cranley Place and Cranley Gardens. With these, Freake had also planned a number of mews to service these "spacious and handsome family residences", one being Cranley Mews and another, behind Cranley Terrace, was Avenue Close, later Sydney Close and Sydney Mews.

above Warwick Square Mews.

above Sumner Place Mews.

left Onslow Mews West – past and present.

These are but a few of the many speculators and builders who have shaped and moulded the texture of London. Effectively, they had set out to make money but, with the collaboration of the wealthy and architecturally minded landowners, they had ended up transforming fields and pastures into buildings and superimposing an ordered and classical landscape onto the land, thus insuring a well-deserved place in the city's history.

planning

The idea of large-scale town planning in London only gained momentum after the Great Fire destroyed almost the entire City in 1666. Consequently, various plans were devised for the rebuilding of the capital, amongst them schemes prepared by Christopher Wren and John Evelyn. These plans did not concentrate on merely replacing existing structures and roads, but were based on a completely new way of thinking by architects, artists and engineers that had started to emerge in Renaissance Italy over two centuries earlier. Books such as *The Republic* by Plato and Aristotle's *Politics* inspired new philosophers such as Sir Thomas More accomplished in *Utopia* (1516), to write about life in an ideal city.

However, it was in the writings of an Italian, Leon Battista Alberti, in *Dieci Libri* (1484), that the idea of a complete urban unit – the "ideal city" – had been created. Alberti, the first of many such theorists, believed that:

> ...a City is not built wholly for the sake of Shelter, but ought to be so contrived that besides more Civil conveniences there may be handsome Spaces left for Squares, Courses for Chariots, Gardens, Places to take the Air in, for swimming, and the like, both for Amusement and Recreation.

Wren formulated his plan around these same architectural ideas. The Royal Exchange and St Paul's Cathedral occupy prominent positions with streets of varying widths radiating out from them, thus signifying their importance. In doing so, Wren appeared to have been strongly influenced by an engraving of a proposal for the Piazza Del Popolo in Rome. The remainder of this plan has then been superimposed with an almost rectangular grid of streets. At some of the intersections, piazzas or rond-points have been formed with the hope of creating vistas down the grand streets towards an interesting focal point. To the west, there is an octagonal layout, with a central piazza, reminiscent of an earlier design for an ideal city, conceived by Giorgio Martini in about 1480.

Evelyn, on the other hand, a wealthy, educated and much travelled nobleman, had proposed a different plan composed of a series of open spaces, often containing or flanked by buildings of great importance as with St Paul's, the Lord Mayor's House and the Guildhall, connected with a regular, geometric pattern of streets. Evelyn was also interested in creating a "rhythm" in the grid so neither are the "open spaces" of the same size "nor should these be all of them square, but some of them oblong, circular, and oval figures, for the better grace and capacity."

right Marylebone as seen from the air. The mews can be clearly seen running parallel behind the main streets and Marylebone Lane (bottom middle) meanders across the uniform pattern and "many of these erstwhile rows of stables have been converted into most desirable dwellings"[13]

13 Gordon Mackenzie, *Marylebone – Great City north of Oxford Street*, 1972

Neither of these grand schemes was ever built but, as we have already established, it is possible to see an excellent example of smaller scale town planning, the type that was to influence the composition of London long after the Fire, when the first of the Great Estates, owned by the Earl of Bedford, was developed by Inigo Jones.

Based around a central piazza, it was designed as a complete, almost self-sufficient, unit with accommodation provided for all sections of society, both rich and poor, and, like any other village or small town, containing a church and a market – "segregation, social and functional, took place between street and street, not between estate and estate". This was soon followed by what

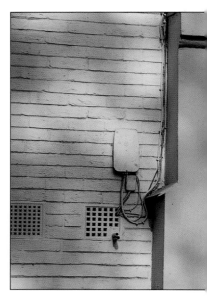

right The entrance to the Colonnade – a run-down mews in Bloomsbury.

above Ennismore Gardens
Mews.

is regarded as being the original London square, the Earl of Southampton's development – Bloomsbury Square – or a "little town" as Evelyn wrote in 1665. This new urban pattern would now be used by the landowners, and their architects, of the many other developing London estates as a planning blueprint for over two hundred years. Donald J Olsen comments that "the distinguishing quality of town planning in the British Isles is its combination of neoclassical façades with a profusion of semi-formal open spaces".[14]

London was essentially a collection of villages. Some would say that it still is today, although the general urban sprawl masks the now almost undetectable boundaries to all but the residents themselves. In part, these villages made up the land that was owned by one or another of the Great Estates and would be the subject of great building projects as the growing need for expansion pushed the perimeter of London further westwards. This land was owned by wealthy and influential private families who were keen to profit both financially and socially from the development of their estates, as Lord Southampton had done in 1661. Financially, because they would use the leasehold system of land tenure thereby insuring not only a limited capital outlay but a continual income derived from the ground rents in the future and the prospect of the buildings and land reverting back to them when the leases expired. Socially, because they hoped that the grand schemes that were subsequently planned and laid out would bring dignity and honour to the names of their families. What is also a significant factor in terms of town planning and why these landlords have had such a great influence on the development of London, was the size of their estates. We only concentrated on a few of the most important earlier in this chapter, and yet between them, their combined lands make up most of what is now considered to be the heart of central London. It was John Gwynn, in his book *London and Westminster Improved* (1766), who worried about the power commanded by these great estates and suggested that London should be planned as a whole rather than by individuals, such as landlords and builders. But his ideas about planning, which included new streets and squares, far from being Utopian, were mostly implemented, and often by the "ignorant and capricious persons" he had once scorned.

London's growth since the Fire has not been continuous. It has been influenced by both political and economic factors as well as the alternation between periods of peace and war. Growth has also been affected by variations of landlord to landlord, from estate to estate. They were never planned to form one expanding mass. Rather, they were developed separately, with no reference to each other, the landowner having his own perception about the character and architectural style that should be imposed on his estate, even

14 Donald J Olsen, *Town Planning in London*, 1982, page 18

down to the class of tenant that he wished to attract by the use of the combination of different rates of house that would be built. As most of the estates are contiguous with at least one other, it is only when the land has been built out and developed to its extremities, or a decisive event manifests itself such as a tactful marriage or the construction of a new arterial road, that a relationship is formed with another estate.

Olsen suggests that there are three stages of town planning – "building, preservation and rebuilding"– and this is correct for the majority of the estates as they developed from country to town and remains true today. London is constantly in a state of transformation, as ideas and technology change, and building works can be seen in almost every street, with scaffolding on many houses.

However, the planning of the London estates had to be functional, as well as architecturally pleasing, due to the increasing use of the horse and carriage as a practical means of transport from the sixteenth century onwards. The typology was altered, from meandering lanes to streets that were wide and straight in order to facilitate rapid progress through the town. The architecture was transformed as the buildings could then be seen from a greater distance. The façades became more monumental in the great squares that were being developed. This "architecture of the carriageway" was to have a noticeable impact on the shape of London. The basic principle of the landowner was to attract a fashionable and respectable class of tenant to the estate, and with the influx of these new tenants came the need to accommodate the great number of horses and carriages that came with them. The mews were a natural progression from the private stables and livery yards that had previously been used and were now intimately connected with the design of the London house. The ordered grid of streets that was emerging meant that the mews could be easily and discreetly contained behind the houses in the main square or street and in the most exclusive areas each house had its own mews house to the rear. The carriages could be called to the front when needed but would otherwise be kept out of sight. These new dwellings fitted into the idea of the "little town", where the master and servant lived in relatively close proximity and yet occupied completely diverse worlds. The mews, as a separate entity, was formed – the cobbled lanes provided for the horses and ease of drainage; the houses were generally built over two storeys. There was no need to build any higher – the ground floor being occupied by the horse and carriage, the first floor as living quarters for the groom, coach driver and other stable hands.

We now come to probably the single most important influence that has affected the architecture and the planning of London since the time of the Great Fire.

classicism

It was in 1715, during the reign of George I, that the classical revival gained momentum with two books; *Vitruvius Britannicus* published by Colen Campbell and Palladio's *Quattro Libri* published by Giacomo Leoni. Certainly, as we have already seen, classical designs and motifs had already been implemented in the middle of the seventeenth century by Inigo Jones, who had also studied the writings and buildings of Andrea Palladio (1508-80) and who heralded the Renaissance in England in the design of the piazza at Covent Garden which "represented all that was correct in the classical Italian architecture he was translating to the streets of London – coherence, uniformity, proportioning and elegance in spite of the simplicity and repetition used in his design".[15] Georgian architecture was to be strongly influenced by Palladio's *Quattro Libri*, and he had in turn been influenced by an even earlier work, that of Vitruvius in his treatise *De Architectura*, written in 20 AD.

below An engraving of the Royal Stables at Charing Cross on the site of the present National Gallery.

It was the young patron, the third Earl of Burlington (1694-1753), who vitalised the English Palladian movement, which lasted for approximately the next forty-five years. In 1715, he was just twenty-one but already had a keen interest in architecture and had recently travelled to Italy. He proceeded to develop his estate behind Burlington House assisted by Colen Campbell (1673-1729) and Giacomo Leoni (c 1686-1746). He then revisited Italy on a Grand Tour and returned in 1719 along with his protegé William Kent (1685-1748).

It was Kent who produced an initial scheme for the redevelopment of the Royal Mews at Charing Cross in 1731, with a budget from the Treasury of £6,500. This was the first in an ambitious catalogue of public and governmental buildings that the English Palladian movement had planned, and amongst their numbers were the most prominent architectural figures at that time – William Chambers (1723-96) and Robert Adam (1728-92). However, the King was not satisfied with the proposal. Kent revised the façade using what became the standard motif for important and grand stables, the "diocletian window". However, it was Burlington who had first used this device – a semicircular window divided into three lights by two vertical mullions – in 1723. The idea was derived from the Thermae of Diocletian in Rome, probably seen by Burlington when he published Palladio's drawings of Roman thermae in 1730, and from Palladio's designs for churches, including San Giorgio Maggiore in Venice, which was one of the subjects in Kent's *Designs of Inigo Jones* published three years earlier. The design was simple yet effective, allowing just the right amount of light to penetrate the walls of the stable on the inside whilst retaining the integrity of the classical façade on the outside. For the interior, Kent looked for inspiration to the stables at Holland House, thought to be the work of Inigo Jones. Unfortunately, only one section of the Royal Mews was ever completed and has since been demolished.

below Detail of the nave of Palladio's San Giorgio Maggiore in Venice showing the use of diocletian windows.

below An engraving of the stables at Holland House in Kensington.

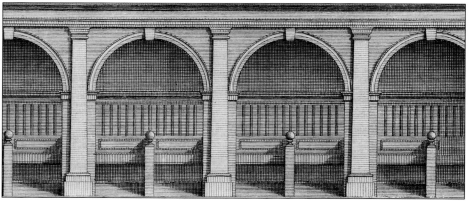

In 1762, George III bought Buckingham House with its own private stables. The mews remained at Charing Cross until they became too cramped to accommodate the increasing number of horses and carriages belonging to the King. It was decided to move some of the entourage to the existing stables behind Buckingham House, now to be known as the Royal Mews Pimlico. It was only in the reign of George IV that John Nash, the King's favourite architect, was appointed to remodel Buckingham House and rebuild the Royal Mews. The site was a rather awkward shape hemmed in between a number of houses at the rear of Buckingham Palace but Nash managed to place a large quadrangle in the centre. This inner court was approached from the south under a triumphal Doric arch, with a matching arch on the north side. The coaches were housed on the east side, and on the west were the stables and harness rooms. The living quarters for the staff were, as usual, on the first floor.

As well as the Royal Mews, Nash was responsible for the stables and coach-houses behind Carlton House Terrace. Designed in 1829-32, the mews has sadly now been demolished.

right Carlton Mews, designed by John Nash (now demolished).

above The double ramp leading to the stables on the first floor.

Classicism was not reserved just for grand schemes but was also to be found on a more domestic scale, as development on the large estates escalated. It can be seen in the uniform and regular, often opulent, terraces which constitute the squares and crescents – features so typical of Georgian London – by architects such as James Burton, John Nash, George Basevi and the Cubitts. Set behind these main thoroughfares were the mews. The houses situated in these lanes were never originally designed to be seen but were purely functional having none of the airs and graces of their larger and grander neighbours. The landlords of the great estates and developers were keen to introduce them, often in great numbers, but were not concerned about their aesthetic or architectural qualities. A suitable analogy can be made between London, in the eighteenth and nineteenth centuries, and an orchestra. The "composer" of the score is the landlord, who determines the style and quality of the environment with his experience and knowledge. The "conductor" is the speculator who translates and articulates the landlord's ideas into reality. If the buildings are the "orchestra", then the grand schemes of Bedford, Grosvenor and Portland are the important first and second violins, and the mews represent the percussion – necessary to assist the more superior instruments and always playing a part in the whole arrangement, no matter how small, but rarely heard in isolation.

above Formally no. 19 Grosvenor Square, the classical garden front of stable building provides an agreeable outlook for the occupants of the main house.

left No 17 Kensington Square, garden front to stable building – note the balustrading and the diocletian windows on the ground floor.

In relation to the mews, classical motifs only really appear when the idea of a decorative arched entrance was introduced on some estates, predominantly in Belgravia and South Kensington. This was a fashion set by Nash in his treatment of the Royal Mews and the mews behind the terraces in Regent's Park. The garden façades of some mews houses in Mayfair and Kensington also provide an excellent example of ornate classical design which only accentuates the conflict between what the occupants of the main houses wished to see from their windows and private terraces and the plain and modest elevations of the cottages that are viewed from the mews side. However, with the increased popularity of these former stables being converted into homes, the last few decades have seen classical idioms utilised merely as a pastiche, with decoration and ornamentation, such as porticoes, pediments and balustrades, used to gentrify the façade of the mews house.

decline

After the frenzied developments by speculators on the great estates in the eighteenth and early nineteenth centuries, the number of mews under construction was still escalating even up to the latter part of the nineteenth century. But if the initial process of transforming land from pastures and swamps into fashionable areas with open streets and squares was an arduous and long-winded process for both the landlord and the builder, then the demise and general decline of a number of the estates, together with the mews, was relatively quick. This alteration came about for two reasons.

left Colbeck Mews.

Firstly, the expansion of London produced a ripple-in-a-pond effect. As new areas such as Mayfair, Westminster and Kensington were developed, so the upper-classes migrated into them leaving behind the elegant squares and streets, such as those of the once fashionable Bloomsbury, to slide into commercial use and, the burden of every landlord, multi-occupation by the poor with most of the grand mansions converted into tenements. The demand for stables in these areas had been over-estimated and thus the mews degenerated, being "more generally occupied by poor families carrying on little trades, and by profligate and destitute persons, than as stables."[16] In Charles Booth's map of London in 1889, where every street was allocated a different colour varying from yellow, the wealthiest, to black, the poorest, all the mews on the Bedford Estate were coloured pink – denoting "working-class comfort". In contrast, stables were still required as late as the 1880s by the large houses in Kensington, which had now reached its fashionable peak, in particular the area surrounding Cornwall Gardens and further south on the Gunter Estate where a considerable number of mews were built: Wetherby Mews (1871-5), Morton Mews (1875-8), Colbeck Mews (1876-84) and the "biggest and finest", Hesper

left and below The former stables and coach-house built in 1882-3 by James Brooks for the Marquis of Londonderry. No 11 Brick Street is described architecturally, which is a very rare for a mews, as being "…red brick with rubbed brick and terracotta dressings, slate roof with high stacks on front elevation. Courtyard plan, with carriage entrance in centre of front elevation intended to provide ground floor accommodation for the stable hands and a first floor suite for the coachman. Separate block to right formally housing loose-boxes, with coach-house to rear. Narrow range to left originally also stables. Street elevation of seven bays with central carriage entrance under terracotta Gibbs surround with decorated keystone and three-light terracotta oriel. Double doors with decorative ironwork in open panels. Circular window to right, the other fenestration comprise eight and twelve-light sashes under segmental heads with keystone. To the rear of this block elaborate Dutch gables with pyramidal tops, that to centre with moulded brick niches and the arms of the Marquis of Londonderry."[17]

16 Foundling Estate Paving Commission Minutes, 1997 page 4

17 The Department of National Heritage – Schedule TQ2880SE (Source: *The Builder*, 17 February 1883, page 207)

right Elgin Mews North (1981).

right Alba Place (1880).

Mews (1884-5). But even here, the number of mews exceeded demand. The ripple that had begun in the early 1700s had finally caught up with these last outposts of wealth and the mews, in their original form, were left behind.

Secondly, as early as 1829, the omnibus had been established in London. This meant that not only could people live further away from where they worked but, with the constantly improving communications network, the need to keep private carriages with horses and grooms, by all but the very rich, who refused to use public transport, diminished. With the even more influential advent of the motor-car and the Underground, London expanded still further, creating new suburbs for the middle-classes and subsequently the need to supply stables in conjunction with housing projects was virtually extinguished. This rapid change in London's typology was both social and economic and lasted well into the twentieth century.

below Clarges Mews (1969).

left Moreton Terrace Mews (1979).

conversion

These changing conditions left the vast majority of the mews without any real purpose or identity. It was to be a long time before they were transformed from servants' quarters into the smart addresses and, in this interim period, most deteriorated into a state of dilapidation and were being occupied by people who could not afford to live anywhere else and invariably including a motley selection of "back-street" trades. There is no evidence as to exactly when these properties were converted from stables and coach-houses to homes, but the estates were keen to remedy this unfortunate situation. The Grosvenor Estate initiated a rebuilding programme of a number of their often substantial stables and coach-houses in mews such as Adam's Row, Mount Row and Three Kings Yard. It was unfortunate that this general improvement came just before the "gradual eclipse of the horse by the motor car". Coach-houses were now converted into garages, and even today the mews are firmly connected with the motor trade, lending themselves to repair shops and car showrooms. It was shortly after this that the idea of converting the stables into dwelling houses was first mooted and the consequences of this critical decision entirely altered the perception of the "mews house", an expression which is still very much in evidence today.

right Drayson Mews is almost entirely taken up with car workshops and showrooms.

right Clabon Mews – note the brick arches representing the former coach-house doors.

above Aldford Street – in 1915 it was home to what was considered to be the "best *bijou* house in London".

The *Survey of London* indicates that one of the first examples of this new style was the adaptation, in 1908, of No 1 Streets Mews (now no 2 Aldford Street), in Mayfair, from a stable into a "dwelling house" and goes on to comment, "By 1910 tenants on the estate were said to have a general desire to get rid of horses." It was in 1915 that Edmund Wimperis, then the surveyor of the Grosvenor Estate, pointed out the apparent success of this conversion, potentially "making it the best *bijou* house in London". After the First World War, there was an increasing number of conversions taking place and redundant stables and coach-houses in Mount Row, Shepherd's Place, Lees Place, Blackburne's Mews and Culross Street were "replaced by modest dwellings, each intended for single-family occupation". In 1923, *Country Life* cites an example of such a conversion at No 1 Mount Row by the architects, Gilbert and Constanduros.

Just as there had once been a need for the speculator and architect when the great estates were first being developed, there now emerged a new breed of builder who was to use the existing structures, mainly stables and coach-houses, in the mews and convert them into houses. This solved the problem of any unwanted or unnecessary dilapidation and it was relatively easy to adapt these "equine palaces" to domestic use for those "no longer willing or able to live in a great house in one of the fashionable streets". After Wimperis retired in 1928, the architect, Frederick Etchells, had established himself as the "monarch of the mews". Other names that were prominent in this fruitful period of mews conversion are Stanley-Barrett and Driver, who were responsible for work in Balfour Mews and further west in Gasper Mews and Lanconia Mews (now De Vere Cottages), where the *Survey of London* describes them as being "architects fertile in mews conversions in Kensington".

above No 3 Lees Place, originally the stables to No 23 Grosvenor Square, in 1890 and 1976. The exterior of this converted coach-house was recently used to portray a grand London house in the cult American television series *Friends*.

above from left Tudor House in Mount Row, Frederick Etchells, 1929-31. Wren House in Mount Row, TP Bennett, 1926-7. De Vere Cottages, Stanley-Barrett and Driver, 1918-25.

right Converted eighteenth-century stables in Nightingale Lane.

left No 10 South Eaton Place and **right** No 10 Minera Mews – although the majority of mews houses are now sold independently to the houses they once served, there is an increasing demand for large properties, particularly in Belgravia and Mayfair, with ancillary accommodation – and even rarer to find corresponding numbers. The grooms have been replaced by chauffeurs, the horse and carriage replaced by the car and so the traditional function of the mews house, albeit a more up-to-date version, has been revived.

The conversion of the mews house into living accommodation occurred at a similar time to the conversion of the main houses they had once served into flats and maisonettes. Not only was this metamorphosis due to the replacement of the horse and carriage by mechanised transport but also can be attributed to the escalating cost of maintaining live-in staff in the large private residences. In the 1920s, it was reported by some newspapers that the smart inhabitants of these new conversions did not employ maids – "no room for one and no need for one."

The popularity of the mews house, with differing elements of society, increased after the Second World War. In the 1950s, the "raffish element crept in".[18] In the 1960s, "radical chic had arrived".[19] And by the 1970s, the age of the mews house as an acceptable, and even desirable, form of accommodation was firmly ensconced in the fabric of London, a condition that is affirmed in the 1990s and hopefully will continue to be regarded as such well into the next millennium.

18 Nick Foulkes, *A talent to a mews*, The Evening Standard Magazine, July 1993, page 50

19 Gerald Cadogan, *Short on space but big on charm*, The Financial Times, 21/22 June 1997, page xv

conservation

Even as recently as the 1970s, there were still a great number of mews houses in central London that had not yet been converted into residential accommodation and remained, to a certain extent, in their original state, as loose boxes and stabling for horses. Those that had been redeveloped often paid little or no attention to the historical or architectural context of the mews. The original detailing had been cast off – replaced by PVC bow windows and mass-produced double-glazed units; "Georgian" style front doors, porches and pediments; false shutters; metal electronic up-and-over garage doors; mean and fiddly ironwork; and a variety of totally unsuitable and incongruous cladding materials and paint finishes.

It was only towards the end of the 1970s and the beginning of the 1980s, when the idea of conservation became more popular and socially acceptable, that the City of Westminster and the Royal Borough of Kensington and Chelsea initiated design guidelines for the alteration of mews houses by the owners and their architects, although the Grosvenor Estate had established conservation policies in the 1960s. These two London boroughs not only contain the majority of the surviving mews in the capital but also some of the finest examples. The Planning and Transportation Department of Westminster City Council produced one such booklet in 1983 entitled *Mews – A Guide to Alterations* which states in its introduction that it "regards mews as a valuable asset, the traditional character of which should be preserved or enhanced, by preventing insensitive alterations and needless demolition". It

above Ensor Mews showing the original Collinge hinges. These hinges are still manufactured today by Charles Collinge and Co Ltd and are often used in architecturally sensitive designs.

below Queen's Gate Mews.

goes on to discuss the appropriate criteria for the retention of roof-lines, façades, windows and doors, architectural features and street surfaces. Retrospective conservation is also encouraged where possible and "the opportunity taken to restore the original appearance where earlier inappropriate alterations have taken place". Over the years, the character of the mews has often been enhanced by the variety of uses contained in the street. Queen's Gate Mews typifies this category where some properties are used as garages and workshops, some have been converted into residential

below Elnathan Mews.

accommodation and others replaced by new houses. There is a public house, an up-market car showroom and, until recently, there was a Shell petrol station, built on the site of London's first petrol pump established in 1913. According to the Royal Borough of Kensington and Chelsea this "variety makes an important contribution to the local economy and is certainly not incompatible with conservation area status."

Whilst there are only sixty-two listed mews buildings in London, a great deal more lie within Conservation Areas, such as Ennismore Gardens Mews and Wilton Row, or are controlled by the historic London estates, including Grosvenor, Cadogan and Howard de Walden, which might even draw up their own proposals for any improvements and alterations required. The purchaser would then have to enter into an Agreement with the landlord to carry out these works within a specified timescale before a new lease is granted – a similar pattern to that experienced when the estates were first created by the speculative builder in the eighteenth and nineteenth centuries. However, with the recent and dramatic changes in property legislation, most notably leasehold enfranchisement when the owner of a property can, under certain circumstances, acquire the freehold from the landlord, the grip that the

estates hold over the environment of the mews diminishes and it will soon be only good taste and common sense that will prevail.

The desire to maintain the form and rhythm of the mews is evident not only in individual mews houses but where whole mews have been redeveloped in order to prevent further decay, dilapidation and, at worst, demolition. An excellent example of this type is Grosvenor Crescent Mews which was virtually rebuilt behind the existing façades by the Grosvenor Estate to provide both residential and commercial accommodation. Elnathan Mews, on the other hand, is an entire mews built in 1990, comprising of forty-six "mews style" houses, which recreates the traditional ambience and character of the mews, without the obvious disadvantage that mews houses were never actually designed to be lived in, that has now become so fashionable and commercially successful.

The next chapters examine the features, both past and present, that make up the unique architectural character and unusual environment of the mews – the arches, the exteriors, the details, the interiors and concluding with the significant rôle that they play in the life of modern London.

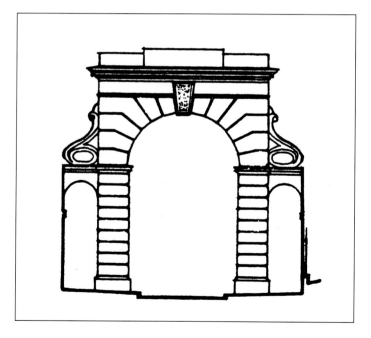

arches

left Four classical arches in South Kensington. Clockwise from top left: Stanhope Mews West. Stanhope Mews East. Stanhope Mews West. Manson Mews.

entrance

There are four types of treatment of the apertures leading to a mews: in the eighteenth century it was merely a simple visual transition by the narrowing of the entrance to the mews; by turning a corner so the mews itself was directly shielded from the sight of passers-by; or an entrance arch incorporated into one bay in the elevation of a terrace of houses. Then by the nineteenth century, the fashion, originated by Nash in the design of the Royal Mews and his work in Regent's Park, introduced the grand and ornate mews arch as an independent element in the street façade, and its prolific use can be seen in the majority of mews in Belgravia and Kensington.

above Montagu Mews North.

From the humble... to the grand... to the modern.

below from left Normand Mews.
Devonshire Row Mews.
Pencombe Mews.

influence

Classical motifs dominated mews arch design from a simple opening to an imposing portal. The basic composition was an aedicule – "the architectural frame of an opening consisting usually of two columns supporting an entablature and pediment."[20] A compendium of other devices were also employed: keystones, rustication, imposts, cornices, pedestals, parapets, orders and scrolls. The Roman Triumphal Arch was also used for inspiration, including the largest and most important Arch of Septimus Severus and the Arch of Constantine in Rome. They are noted for "the most elementary fact of all about them – the division of space by columns into three unequal parts: narrow, wide, narrow, is perhaps also the most important."[21] The arch at the west entrance to Holland Park Mews is probably the best example and "reflects the imposing grandeur of the triumphal arch most closely."[22]

above The Arch of Constantine in Rome.

right The entrance to Holland Park Mews.

20 Sir John Summerson, *The Classical Language of Architecture*, 1996, page 122

21 Sir John Summerson, *The Classical Language of Architecture*, 1996, page 24

22 Anne Riches, *London Mews Arches*, Architectural Review, April 1972

above A gate house at the entrance to Grosvenor Crescent Mews.

context

The mews arch was designed to maintain the integrity and rhythm of the terrace when the idea of the monumental façade was introduced to the planning of streets and squares, most notably Belgrave Square and its environs. The scale is smaller but the language is the same. Elements from the surrounding buildings are utilised in the arch to reflect the imposed grandeur. It is ironic though that the arch, normally associated with an expectation of importance beyond, should be used to signify what are basically servants residences and stables. The view, however, is essentially external. Whilst the street side of the arch is ornate and flamboyant, the mews side is generally left bare – the decoration is only superficial. It is these qualities that now attract the new mews-dweller with the suggestion that they are entering an exclusive domain, under a ritual arch, rather like passing through a gate-house on the way to a secluded country retreat.

opposite The Gothic arch at the north entrance of Pont Street Mews inscribed with the date "1879". The mews itself is a tranquil crescent surrounding St Saviour's Church on Walton Street and yet just a stone's throw from the hustle and bustle of Harrods.

left Berghem Mews – a modern interpretation of the classical arch.

overleaf Behind the north terrace of Cadogan Square lies Shafto Mews, named after the barrister John Eden Shafto, with its symmetrical red-brick façade. The central arch in the "Pont Street Dutch"[23] style is reminiscent of church elevations in the sixteenth century, most commonly found in Italy, with the classical pediment flanked by scrolls, which are also visible in the protruding chimney stacks either side.

23 Osbert Lancaster, *Pillar to Post*, 1983, page 54

Belgrave Mews South.

Belgrave Mews North.

Belgrave Mews West.

Chester Square Mews.

Belgrave Mews West.

Grosvenor Crescent Mews.

Eccleston Mews.

Lyall Mews West.

Lyall Mews.

Eaton Mews South.

Eaton Mews West.

Eaton Mews West.

Grosvenor Gardens Mews East.

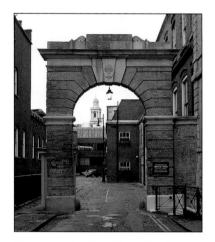

Grosvenor Gardens Mews North.

Eaton Mews North.

Headfort Place.

Lowndes Close.

Roberts Mews.

previous pages Belgravia –
classical arches dominate the
mews on the Grosvenor Estate,
the design of many being
attributed to the builder,
Thomas Cubitt.

right The forlorn entrance arch
of Stanhope Mews East is often
missed as the seemingly endless
flow of traffic rushes along the
busy Cromwell Road.

left Harrington Gardens –
two classical arches remain
although the mews are no longer
recognisable. To the north (**left**)
is the arch once leading to
Grenville Mews, now used by
the Gloucester Hotel as ancillary
accommodation; to the south
(**below**) is an equally elegant arch
leading to a hidden courtyard
and retaining its iron gates.

right One of the Doric arches, designed by John Nash in the 1820s, leading to the Royal Mews in the grounds of Buckingham Palace.

left Devonshire Place Mews.

below Kynance Mews.

above Albert Mews.

right Osten Mews.

above Lexham Mews

above Laverton Mews.

left Cornwall Mews South.

above Garden Mews.

right Fulton Mews.

left and below The arch to Queen's Gate Place Mews (c1855), which is Grade II listed, is of a complex classical design consisting of a large central opening, presumably to accommodate grand carriages, with two smaller pedestrian entrances either side. The curved pediment, containing an elaborate scrolled motif and entablature are supported by two "giant" Ionic columns, and the elevation is part-rusticated in both smooth and vermiculated styles.

right Ennismore Gardens
Mews.

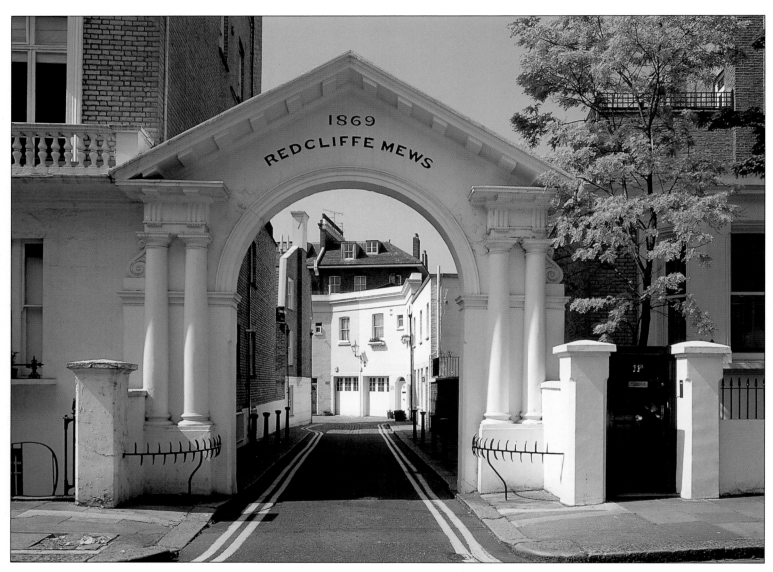

above Redcliffe Mews has only one arched entrance which is constructed from a simple opening flanked by twin Doric columns supporting an entablature and the pediment, and inscribed with the date "1869".

above Elgin Mews North and Elgin Mews South – These Venetian Gothic gate houses form an excellent and original transition to the mews

above Steele's Mews South and (**top**) Steele's Mews North.

right In Courtfield Mews only the bases of the arch remain.

exteriors

left Lennox Gardens Mews
surely must be one of the most
picturesque and well-maintained
mews in London.

above St Luke's Mews.

above Kersley Mews.

character

"The merit of the mews of London is that we are more frequently charmed than shocked."[24]

Once through the entrance the mews can be seen extending into the distance, seemingly unaware of the street scene that has been left behind. Although a mews is almost always instantly recognisable, the type, size and character of the properties vary enormously from area to area. This diversity is not only seen with the original design of the mews houses but with the constant progression of time. The need for change and adaption is woven into the fabric of the city and the different requirements and trends of each new generation have each inflicted their own ideals.

style

The external qualities of mews buildings derive in part from their original function as stables and coach-houses. It is the simplicity of design and use of materials, the apparent uniformity and the strong visual definition between ground and upper floors, with the exaggerated timber bresummers, that contribute to the unique environment of the mews. However, architectural design is not an exact science and subtle variations are noticeable on closer inspection. A number of mews feature external balconies, Dove Mews and Holly Mews, that span the length of a terrace with access to the first floor gained at either end, whilst others, most notably Holland Park Mews and Queensberry Mews West, have steep external staircases that rise up to the first floor on each house.

scale

The secondary importance of the mews is reflected in the scale of the mews houses, being mainly two storey cottages, and the surrounding architecture. In some of the more fashionable areas where the properties they originally served are considerably substantial, it is possible to feel dwarfed by the immediate landscape. The contrast of the brightly painted houses, the rustic individuality and the cobbled lanes serve as a stark comparison with the rear of of these properties which have, unlike their ordered and fastidious street façades, been extended and altered beyond recognition. The view from the mews is essentially that of plain and unadorned brickwork, drainpipes, wires,

above Queensberry Mews West.

above Hesper Mews.

24 Barbara Rosen and Wolfgang Zuckerman, *The Mews of London,* 1982, page 138

left Pembroke Mews – note the rusticated key stones above the first-floor windows and the egg-and-dart moulding under the eaves.

above Ebury Lodge – built on the site of a dilapidated bakery in Ebury Mews.

left Six views of Adam and Eve Mews – this extensive mews lying to the south of Kensington High Street has gone by a number of different titles. Originally called Palace Stables, it then changed to Adam and Eve Stables (after the Adam and Eve public house that had once stood on this site – one of "Kensington's most ancient inns"), appearing on an Ordnance Survey map in 1865 as Adam and Eve Cottages, and finally its present and more familiar name. It is worth noting the interesting pointed gables and cross-brick pattern on a number of the parapet walls, a similar style to that found in Grosvenor Crescent Mews.

above and right Lennox Gardens Mews.

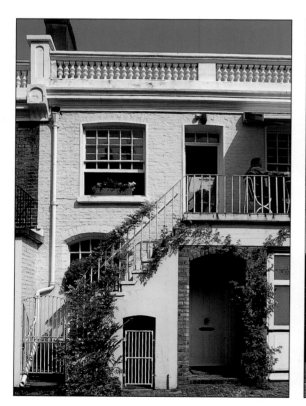

left and below Holland Park Mews is notable for its roof balustrading and the steep external staircases leading to the first floor.

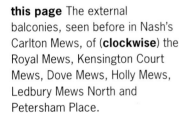

this page The external balconies, seen before in Nash's Carlton Mews, of (**clockwise**) the Royal Mews, Kensington Court Mews, Dove Mews, Holly Mews, Ledbury Mews North and Petersham Place.

above and right A extremely unusual corner house in Hays Mews.

this page The Royal Mews – details of the quadrangle.

Albert Mews – running at an oblique angle to Victoria Grove, this mews has an interesting, if slightly dilapidated, classical arch leading to a narrow and uniform balconied section, with coach-houses on the ground floor and living quarters on the first floor accessed via outside stairs and a full-length external balcony, then opening into a secluded courtyard (**above**). It is one of a number of mews in Kensington that share this distinctive feature.

right Roland Way, originally Alveston Mews until 1921 and then Roland Mews until 1936, features a multitude of rare semi-circular arched stable doors.

right and below Portsea Mews – a small but interesting mews painted in a uniform olive green colour.

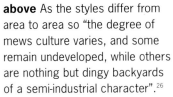

above As the styles differ from area to area so "the degree of mews culture varies, and some remain undeveloped, while others are nothing but dingy backyards of a semi-industrial character".[26]

26 Jeremy Cockayne, *Rooms without views*, Blueprint, February 1990

this page Kynance Mews.

below and right Pont Street
Mews.

Brownlow Mews.

Lyall Mews.

Addison Place.

Cranley Mews.

Thurloe Place Mews.

Wilton Row.

Devonshire Close.

Devonshire Close.

Clabon Mews.

Cheyne Mews.

Horbury Mews.

Addison Place.

Ladbroke Walk.

Ladbroke Walk.

Clabon Mews.

Marylebone Mews.

Hyde Park Gardens Mews.

Doughty Mews.

Hesper Mews.

Doughty Mews.

101

Devonshire Mews South.

Doughty Mews.

Kersley Mews.

Cresswell Place.

St Anselm's Place.

Russell Gardens Mews.

Cromwell Mews.

Osten Mews.

Petersham Mews.

Bathurst Mews.

Groom Place.

Petersham Place.

Ledbury Mews North.

Devonshire Close.

Rosslyn Mews.

Ladbroke Walk.

Woods Mews.

Woods Mews.

Woods Mews.

Wilton Row.

De Vere Cottages.

Hays Mews.

PETROL
VEHICLE TESTING STATION
APPROVED BY
THE DEPARTMENT OF TRANSPORT
DIESELS TESTED
Shell

elements

left Shell sign at the entrance to Queen's Gate Mews. The petrol station, now demolished, was on the site of London's first petrol pump established in 1913.

text

The street-name signs of the mews display a fascinating variety of text, from the historic, such as Mount Row, to the modern, Rutland Mews West, and even to the extent of being proudly cast into the elevation, as with Horbury Mews. These signs are not the only examples of text to appear in the mews. There is also a wealth of other signs and placards from the almost universal "No Parking" notice and the indications, some now almost illegible, at the entrance of the mews of the numerous activities that can be found within, to a number of Blue Plaques denoting famous former residents, the most appropriate being located in Cresswell Place which was once the home of the prolific crime writer Agatha Christie, author of *Murder in the Mews*.

right The distinctive Alfa Romeo sign marks the entrance to Railway Mews.

opposite and following pages A variety of mews name signs.

Palace Garden Mews.

The Royal Mews.

The Royal Mews.

Eaton Mews West.

Elvaston Mews.

Cheyne Mews.

Lucerne Mews.

Montpelier Mews.

Cheyne Mews.

Moreton Terrace Mews North.

Malvern Mews.

Fosbury Mews.

Queens Mews.

Doughty Mews.

Queens Mews.

Rutland Gardens Mews.

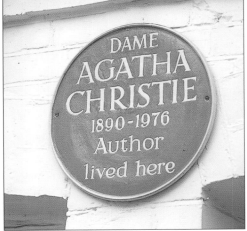

Cresswell Place.

Queen's Gate Mews.

above St Luke's Mews

right A detail of the entrance to Shafto Mews.

texture

The simplicity of exterior design is repeated in the often limited range of construction materials used in the mews. The ground covering usually consists of cobbles or granite setts, unless overlaid with the dreaded tarmac, and the cottages lining the mews give directly onto the street without the benefit of a pavement, having only a crude threshold. The walls are brick, normally being left unrendered if not sometimes brightly painted. Where the original coach-house doors remain, being of heavy timber supported by large wrought-iron hinges, they give an overwhelming sense of solidity and permanence. Another feature particular to the mews is that they appear to be both unseasonal and timeless. The general lack of trees in the mews means that there is very little evidence of the changing seasons taken for granted in the main squares and streets.

below Concrete gutters in Shaftesbury Mews create a very brutalist effect.

this page Exterior details.

Portobello Mews.

Albert Mews.

Wilby Mews.

Pont Street Mews.

Jubilee Place.

Chippenham Mews.

Jay Mews.

Errinsmore Mews.

Elvaston Mews.

Clabon Mews.

Colbeck Mews.

juxtaposition

Although the individual features of the mews are themselves provocative, it is often unexpected and unorthodox compositions that stimulate the imagination. It could in the detail of a door or window, an historic plaque, a street light, a sun-dial, an intricate maze of plumbing, a street sign, an original winch bracket replaced on a new house – to name but a few. The extent to which this character is exploited can stretch from the sublime to the ridiculous, an excellent example being the uncanny likeness of the two white birds perched at the entrance to Dove Mews.

Gate Mews.

Drayson Mews.

Ennismore Mews.

Dove Mews.

Colville Mews.

Spear Mews.

The Royal Mews.

Belgrave Mews West.

Alexander Mews.

Spear Mews.

Ladbroke Walk.

Doughty Mews.

Chippenham Mews.

Codrington Mews.

Pont Street Mews.

Lucerne Mews.

Pont Street Mews.

Holland Park Mews.

Codrington Mews.

Princes Mews.

Ennismore Mews.

Queens Mews.

St Luke's Mews.

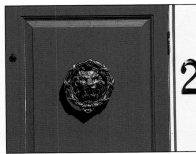
Portobello Mews.

Lennox Gardens Mews.

Relton Mews.

Colville Mews.

Hay's Mews.

Powis Mews.

Kynance Mews.

interiors

space

Although there was some variation in size from area to area, all the mews houses that exist today once conformed to the same ordered pattern. They were all built as stables and coach-houses, they had no rear view or garden, they were generally poorly built (ships' timbers were often used as floor-boards and in the roof as joists) and uncomfortably crowded. The ground floor was taken up with the coach-house, stalls, loose box, harness room and grain bins, the first floor being reserved as sleeping quarters for the coach-men and their families, grooms and other stable staff.

above Stabling in Grosvenor Crescent Mews.

above A horse ramp in De Vere Mews (1972).

right Connolly in Grosvenor Crescent Mews.

transformation

With the advent of motorised transport, the mews house, in its original form, was gradually made redundant and the conversion to predominately residential use began.

The process, established in Mayfair at the beginning of the twentieth century , is now more popular and lucrative than ever with both interior designers and architects. There are however numerous hurdles to overcome, principally due to the physical and structural constraints of the mews house. These can be dealt with on a small scale, with the refurbishment of an individual house, or on a larger scale with either the rebuilding of a group of houses behind their original façades or, where the mews are so dilapidated and beyond repair, the construction of extremely new houses that are sympathetic with their surroundings whilst providing a contemporary environment. Fashions in interior design have also mutated dramatically over the years; from the garish colours and the bold patterns of the 1960s and 1970s to the subtle whites and creams in the luxurious show-homes of the 1990s.

above and left A contemporary conversion in Belgravia by the architects Matthew Preistman/Phillip Tefft.

replacement

One of the most expensive mews houses currently on the market was built on the site of a dilapidated bakery in Ebury Mews. Ebury Lodge, priced at a mere £3,650,000 for an 82-year lease, is a impressive four-storey house designed for Viscount Linley and his wife Serena. With a floor area of over 5300 square feet, it is quite unlike its modest neighbours that have typically retained their original features and identity – although it appears to merge into the mews successfully, apart from the totally unsuitable and incongruous shutters. The accommodation is extensive with a grand first-floor drawing room, a dining room, five bedrooms with en-suite bathrooms, a gymnasium, a courtyard garden and even a staff flat. Included in the price are three elegant mantelpieces from David Linley Furniture in Pimlico Road. Sadly, when it was completed the Linleys never actually took up residence; however, it is sure to make a unique and extremely comfortable home for its future occupants.

left The dining room and (**far left**) detail of one of the David Linley Furniture mantelpieces crafted from light oak with ebony roundels, and (**below**) the courtyard garden.

above The Royal Mews.

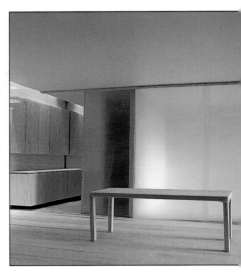

this page A model of a project in Queensbury Mews West designed by the architect Philip Gumuchdjian.

opposite page An elegant mews conversion in Notting Hill.

above This highly imaginative and individual house was designed by the architect, Seth Stein, on the site of a disused stable and builders yard in Kensington. This view, taken from the main living area, shows the central courtyard – some of the brickwork of the original mews building is just visible on the right.

left A view of the dining room – a section of original tiling and wood panelling recovered from the old tack room, can be seen on the back wall.

left and below The interior of a mews house in Ladbroke Walk designed by Nico Rensch.

left Grosvenor Crescent Mews –
as stabling for horses and as
"one of the most beautiful shops
in Europe". Connolly, the luxury
leather goods emporium, was
established in 1878 by two
brothers, Samuel and Joseph
Connolly. Recognition of their
craftsmanship as saddlers was
confirmed when they were
commanded by the Palace to
make the leather seats for the
Coronation Coach of Edward VII.
Connolly, like the mews they
occupy, had to adapt their
skills as transport technology
developed, and the brothers had
to meet the new demands of the
motor car, now producing leather
upholstery for marques such as
Aston Martin, Ferrari and Rolls
Royce. Their premises in
Grosvenor Crescent Mews,
interiors designed Andrée
Putman, were converted from
fire-damaged stables and loose
boxes by the Grosvenor Estate
and admirably reflects Connolly's
170-year history of leather – from
the carriage to the specialist car
industry.

materials

In this quiet Hampstead backwater, an architect has created a unique and modern house in a once aspectless mews. Occupying the entire site, formally a row of run-down mews houses, Blackburn House, in Rosslyn Mews, functions both as a home and an office/gallery for a collection of contemporary furniture, a similar idea to that of the Villa la Roche in Paris, designed by Le Corbusier for a collection of contemporary art. Much of the architecture is revealed by the interior detail – door handles, cantilevered balcony and boat/seat – and the simplicity is enhanced by the use of colour and a carefully selected range of materials.

Architect – Peter Wilson

below Detail of steel bannister with the lighting control box, two-storey sandblasted window giving the occupier only a glimpse at the outside world, the boat/seat.

right The lower living area showing the controlled use of space, materials and colour flooded in natural light.

minimalist

A traditional Victorian cottage in Ennismore Gardens Mews formed the starting point for a "complete restructuring of its interior to transcend the limitations of space and light conventionally associated with homes of this kind". Although there are no features which indicate the history of the property, the project has been imaginatively engineered within the constraints not only of the local conservation area, but within the dimensions of a small cottage with no rear aspect or possibility of extension either horizontally or vertically. The ground floor has been opened up to create a single space. Two functional elements have been introduced – the wall concealing the staircase and another dividing the main room from the kitchen. The first floor has had a similar treatment with the bathrooms contained in a service zone running parallel to the stairs and a single space that can be divided, if necessary, into two bedrooms with the use of folding screens.

Architect – John Pawson

left The bedroom.

below The stairwell with a skylight above.

above The main living area on the ground floor.

office

below View of the interior showing the mezzanine level overhead, the kitchen and the alternating steel steps providing the only slightly precarious access between the levels.

below right External detail of the bedroom which is lit by a wall of sandblasted glass reflecting the mews behind. The more traditional houses of Westbourne Terrace Mews can be seen in the background.

Westbourne Terrace Mews is the location for this dramatic conversion of a garage workshop to a single volume studio space in which the owner could both live and work. The project concentrates on the ground floor of a typical nineteenth-century mews building which has been further excavated to provide additional accommodation on a lower level – kitchen and office. The bedroom is located externally at the front of the property and is lit by a wall of sandblasted glass. The mews elevation has been transformed into a "mobile sculpture" by three full-height pivoting glass doors which can be opened and closed to varying degrees, the impact of which is enhanced, both internally and externally, because the property faces directly down the whole extent of the mews.

Architect – Geoffrey Powis

right The front elevation with the "mobile sculpture" creating a dramatic view of the interior, especially at night.

industrial

Cobham Mews is a triangular site completely surrounded by houses but linked by a cobbled lane – an "umbilical chord"[29] to the main road. It was transformed from an abandoned scrapyard, with none of the familiar characteristics associated with a mews, to a pair of studio offices, one of which is occupied by the architect himself. The desire to create a "small-scale yet interesting space" using rooflights and double height rooms for essentially design orientated businesses – architects, photographers and publishers – whose need for "a characterful and congenial working environment outweighs the necessity for a conspicuous presence in the high street". The design is essentially purist and functional, evoking the villas of Le Corbusier, and the materials used are deliberately simple – exposed concrete, white painted walls, wood block floors, unfinished steel and glass, presenting "an industrial effect which is not unacceptable for a studio".

Architect – David Chipperfield

right A studio.

below The entrance to the studio.

left A detail of a staircase finished in fair-faced concrete.

29 Jeremy Cockayne, *Rooms without views*, Blueprint, February 1990

light

This mews house, in a gated Knightsbridge courtyard, is a "disguised cube" and has been "sculptured internally to create a surprising variety of spaces".[30] The site is tucked into a corner and almost completely enclosed relying on the Victorian idea of "borrowed light." Behind the recessed façade, the vertical circulation and the fluctuation of the horizontal axis, the carefully positioned and proportioned windows and skylights; and the distribution of mass and void contribute to the sense of space, even though most of the rooms are relatively small. The main living area is at the top of the house, with the bedrooms on the ground and first floors, and the treatment of the roof surface allows daylight to penetrate the interior, producing a range of pleasant and subtle deviations to the domestic environment.

Architect – Niall McLaughlin

these pages Views of the 'light fantastic'

30 Hugh Pearman, *Trapping the light fantastic,* The Sunday Times, 26 April 1998

project

Pottery Lane is a winding thoroughfare consisting mainly of private garages and nineteenth-century mews houses. The Project 41 house was designed to be both a home and an office for the art dealer Helen St Cyr, and its striking façade "conceals a triumphant use of vertical space".[31] The interior appears to cascade from the second-floor mezzanine gallery past the first floor, featuring two full-height windows overlooking the well-maintained garden opposite, to the double-height entrance hall. This not only enhances the feeling of space, but adds much needed floor area to what is essentially a small two-storey cottage. There is a sloping glazed roof, with a computer-controlled blind, allowing an abundance of natural light to filter through the building. The internal elements, bathroom, shower room and kitchen, are carefully juxtaposed with dividing walls being designed simply as "coloured planes". The bedrooms are situated on the ground floor with the the first floor defined as the main living area. The owner uses the mezzanine level as a study which, with its distant and appealing views, has now become "a place to work and reflect".

Architect – David Mikhail

right The main living area with the full-height windows overlooking Pottery Lane and the garden opposite.

below The kitchen area with the staircase to the mezzanine level tucked behind and (**right**) the entrance hall and main staircase.

31 Mark Irving, *Magic solution for a London Garage,* The Evening Standard, 5 November 1997

expansion

Having started with one house in Doughty Mews, the owner, an American still-life photographer, commissioned the original architects to further transform the two adjacent units and create a single and suitably imposing triple-fronted house. From the mews, the dark wood stain and intriguing fenestration give the passer-by little insight of the sometimes clinical and light interior which is predominately white with the carefully chosen use of colour reminiscent of the visual simplicity of the Bauhaus and de Stijl. In contrast, the bedroom and study on the second floor evoke the early projects of Le Corbusier, in particular the villa at Garches outside Paris, with the vaulted ceilings and subdued materials, hidden behind the parapet wall which also conceals a full-length roof terrace. A symmetry, both externally and internally, is created with a dominant central studio room, and with its glazed pitched roof provides a versatile source of daylight. This space not only articulates the first floor, acting as a transitional link between the two rooms either side, but is at the heart of the whole building.

opposite Other rooms in Doughty Mews.

right Kitchen.

Study.

Bedroom.

Stairwell.

Studio.

studio

Avenue Studios is an enchanting enclave set behind the Fulham Road. Walking through the entrance arch you step back in time and infiltrate a very private and peaceful setting with tall trees swaying, the high garden walls giving only a glimpse of the grand houses beyond and an assortment of terracotta pots precariously stacked on window sills and brimming with an abundance of colour. Entering the building, the long, partially lit corridor echoes with every cautious footstep. On either side are a range of black doors – daunting and secretive – recalling an image of a row of monks' cells in an ancient monastery. Behind these doors are the studios that have once seen a plethora of prominent artists since they were first built. This particular studio is owned by Conrad and Tricia Jameson whose interests include interior design, an eclectic assortment of rural and horticultural antiques, architectural design and American quilts. The property is dominated by the top-floor studio room with a wonderful north-lit window, polished herringbone parquet floor, muted colours and Gothic stone fireplace. This simplicity of materials and design is repeated in the rest of the house and becomes a perfect backdrop for the apple-pickers' ladders, old watering-cans, bird cages, model horses, paintings, rustic chairs and bunches of dried flowers that decorate the walls.

right The large second-floor studio room.

below View from the mezzanine gallery, model boats, an eclectic assortment of antiques.

"it's a London thing"

The mews certainly is "a London thing"[32]. The photograph on the previous spread taken in 1998 is obviously very different to that of Tavistock Mews a little over a hundred years earlier and yet it encapsulates the entire ethos of what is now "mews style".

There is a tendency to be over nostalgic about the mews, continually recollecting the bygone days of the horse and carriage and the gas lit streets of Victorian London. Yet, as we have seen, the mews can be architecturally current and influential as any form of building. This has not been achieved by ignoring the past but by adapting the present. The mews is the medium, it has fired the imagination and appeals to both the ardent habitué and the casual passer-by intent upon a glimpse into the secluded world. However, this is not the "world" Henry Mayhew originally described in 1851, where the mews were "tenanted by one class – coachmen and grooms, with their wives and families – men who were devoted to one pursuit, the care of horses and carriages" but a world now exploited by a new expression of horsepower – the car. Nonetheless the garages, workshops and showrooms are only part of the narrative. These "village streets inserted into the urban framework"[33] of London are more like John Evelyn's "little town" – they embrace whole communities, irrespective of wealth, culture or occupation. Above all, "mews style" is about a simple dichotomy which appears to divide the citizens of London – those who live and work in the mews, and those who don't!

left Tavistock Mews in 1895 (demolished in 1897).

32 *Tatler about Townies*, The Tatler, July 1998

33 Gordon Mackenzie, *Marylebone – Great City north of Oxford Street, 1972*

34 Gordon Mackenzie, *Marylebone – Great City north of Oxford Street, 1972*

picture credits

Aerofilms Ltd 22, 37

Andreas Von Einseidel 114

Author 54 (top left), 104

British Architectural Library, RIBA, London 42

Christoph Kicherer 129

Connolly, London 98, 116, 124

Country Life Picture Library 43

D.H. Lurot Betjeman vi

David Spero 122

J. Ahlstrom 146

Jeremy Cockayne/Arcaid 13-7

Julian Cornish-Trestail 140-1

Leigh Simpson 123

Nathalie Vidal, Archives Hermès, Paris 3

Nicholas Kane 138-9

Peter Aprahamian 117, 121

Richard Bryant/Arcaid 122, 132-5

Richard Davies 120, 126-7

Richard Glover 128

Sir John Soane's Museum Archives 42

Ssangyong Motor Distributor's Ltd 10

The Royal Collection (c) Her Majesty the Queen 41, 119

Volkswagen UK Ltd/BMP DDB Ltd 6

All other new colour photos - **Bill Burlington**

bibliography

Burke, Gerald – *Towns in the Making*, Arnold, 1986

Byrne, Andrew – *London's Georgian Houses*, The Georgian Press, 1986

Girouard, Mark – *A Sacrifice to the Ladies*, Country Life, January 29 1959

Jenkins, Simon – *The Landlords of London*, Constable, 1975

Lovatt-Smith, Lisa – *London Living*, Weidenfeld and Nicholson, 1997

Mackenzie, Gordon – *Marylebone – Great City north of Oxford Street*, McMillan, 1972

Olsen, Donald J – *Town Planning in London, The Eighteenth and Nineteenth Centuries*, Yale, 1982

Pearman, Robert – *The Cadogan Estate, The History of a Landed Family*, Haggerston Press, 1986

Rasmussen, Steen Eiler – *London, The Unique City*, MIT Press, 1982

Riches, Anne – *London Mews Arches*, Architectural Review, April 1972

Rosen, Barbara and Zuckermann, Wolfgang – *The Mews of London*, Webb and Bower, 1982

Stroud, Dorothy – *The South Kensington Estate of Henry Smith's Charity*, The John Roberts Press, 1975

Summerson, Sir John – *Georgian London*, Penguin, 1991

Summerson, Sir John – *The Classical Language of Architecture*, Thames and Hudson, 1996

Worsley, Giles – *Kent and the Royal Mews*, Country Life, November 12 1987

Worsley, Giles – *London's Greatest Stable*, Country Life, July 24 1986

Much of the information was also collected from the *Survey of London* series including vols XXXVIII (The Museums area of Southern Kensington and Westminster, 1975), XXXIX (The Grosvenor Estate in Mayfair, 1977), XL (The Grosvenor Estate in Mayfair, 1980) and XLI (South Kensington: Brompton, 1983)

index